Reading Is Fun!

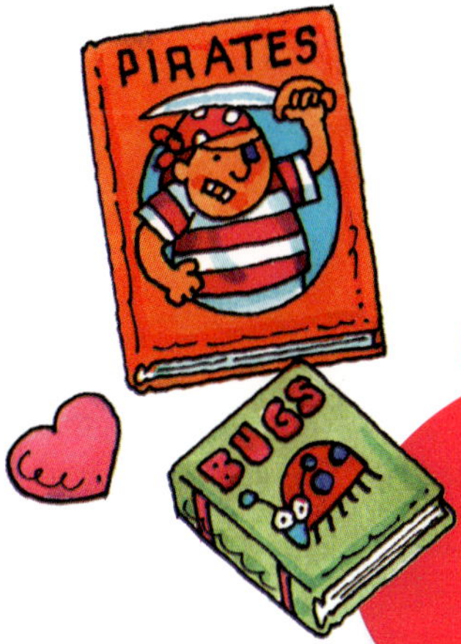

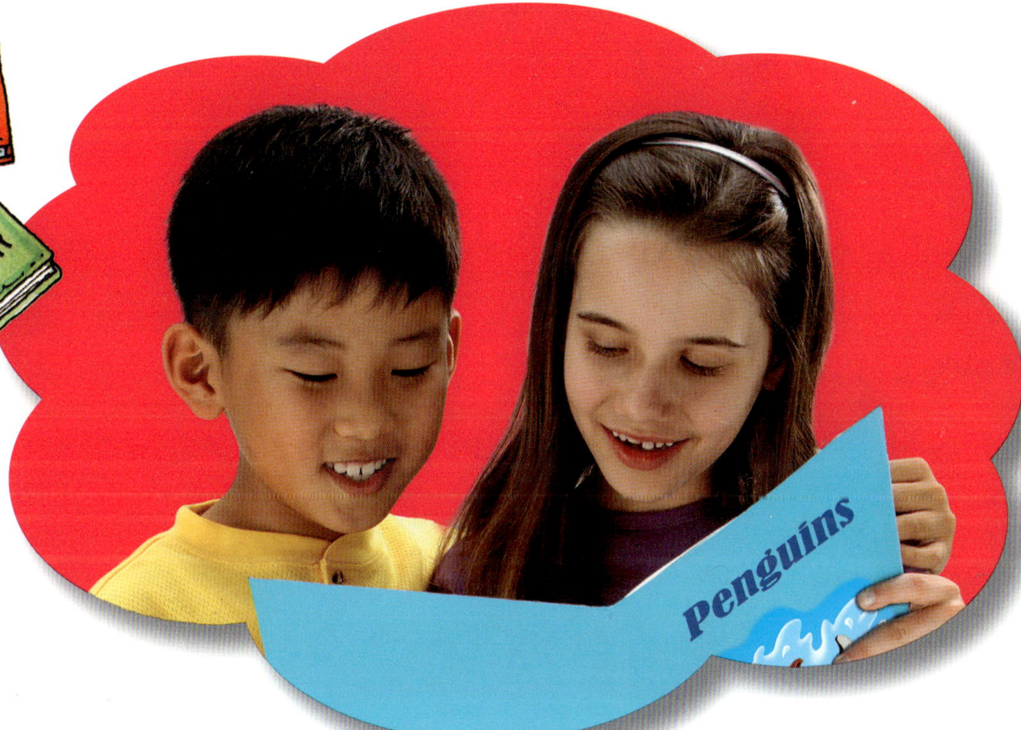

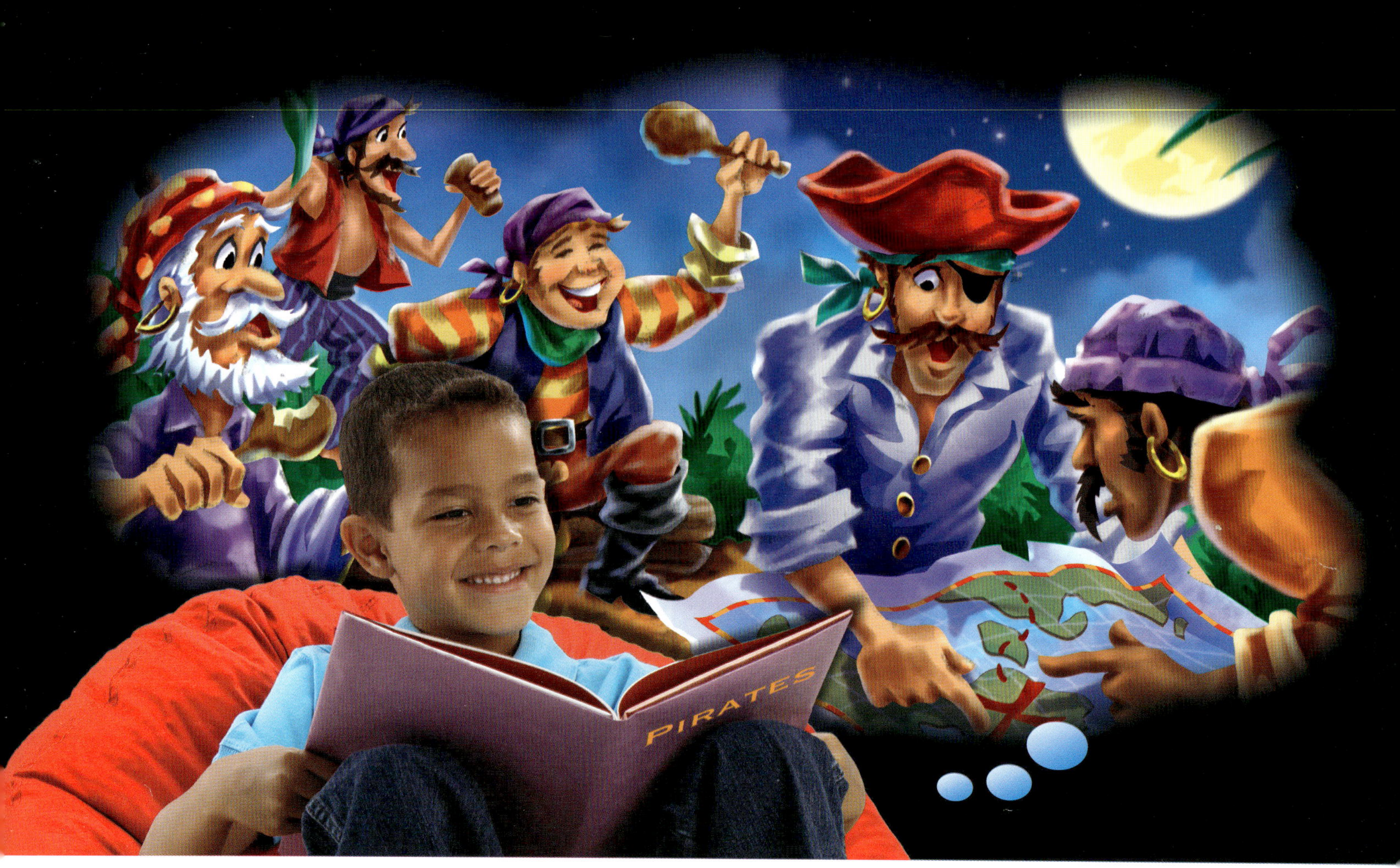

I can read about pirates.

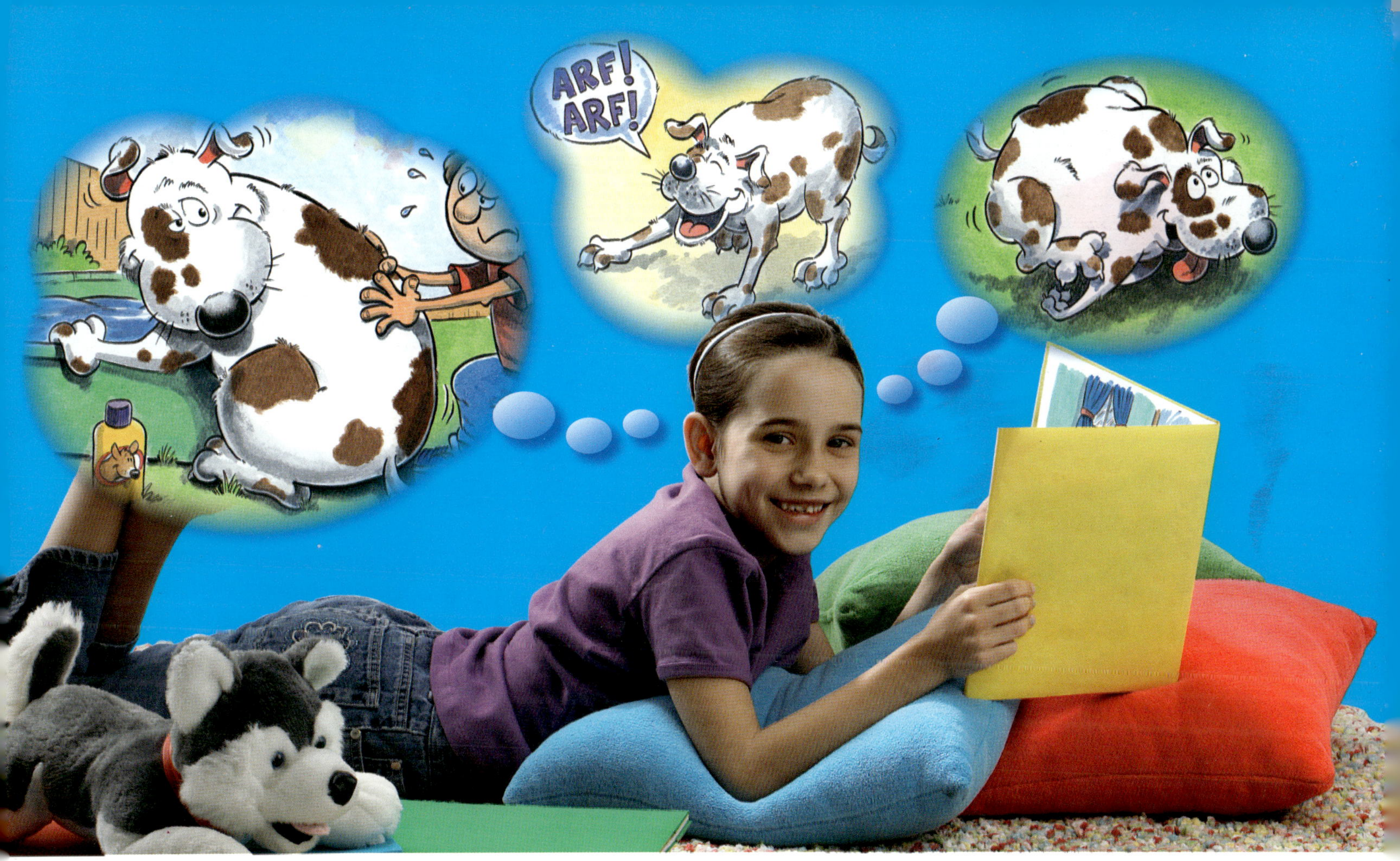

I can read about dogs.

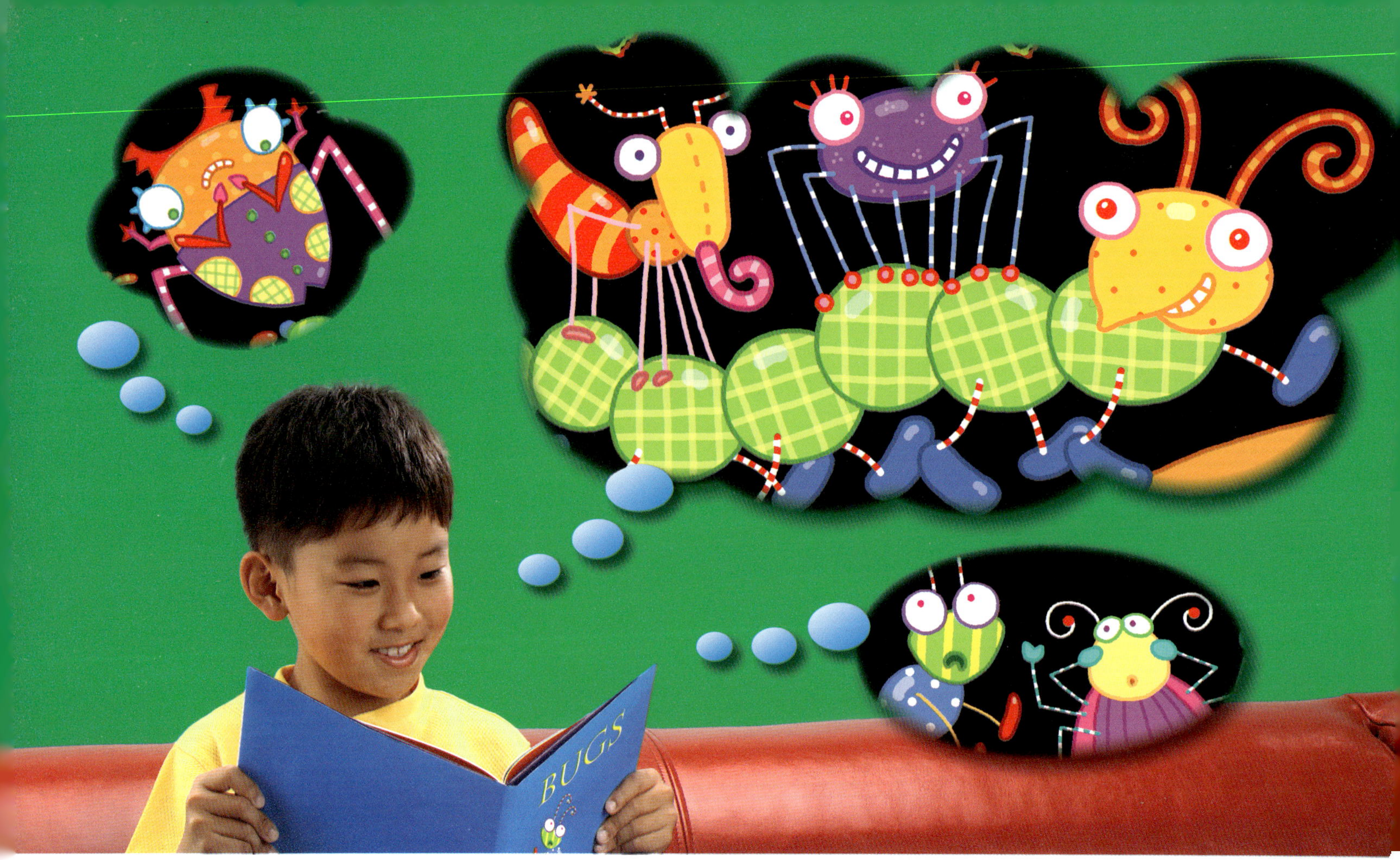

I can read about bugs.

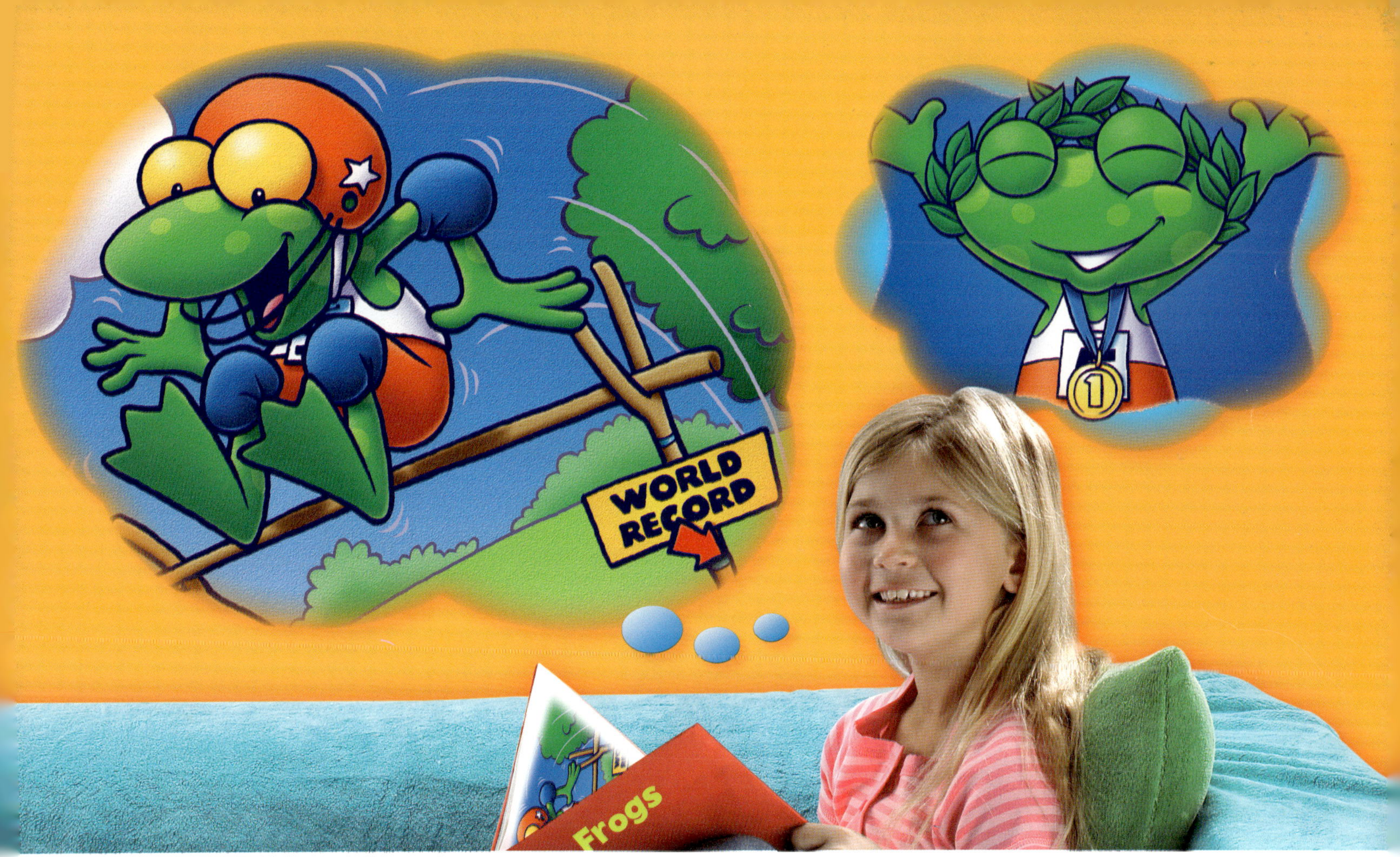

I can read about frogs.

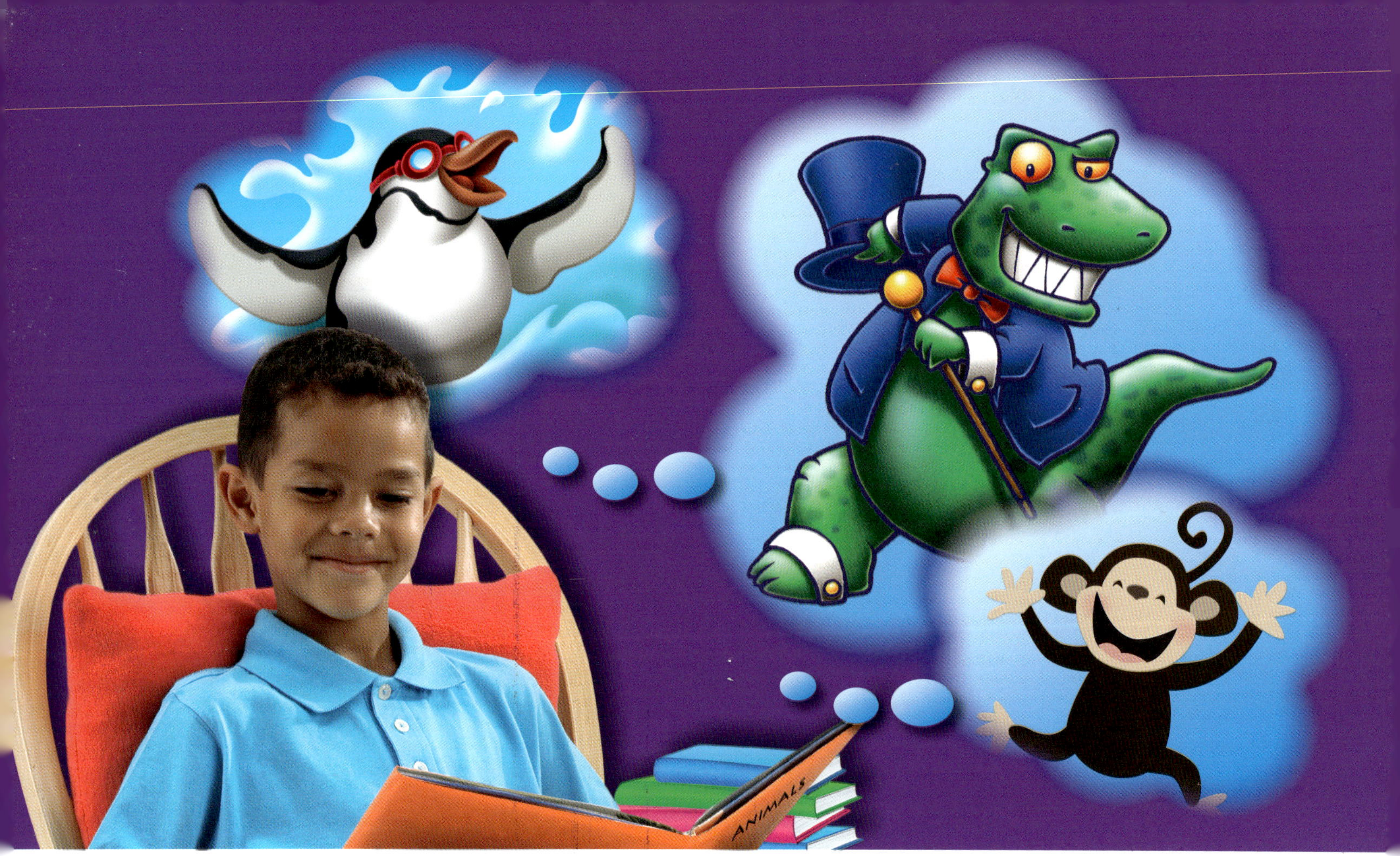

I can read lots of books, not just one.

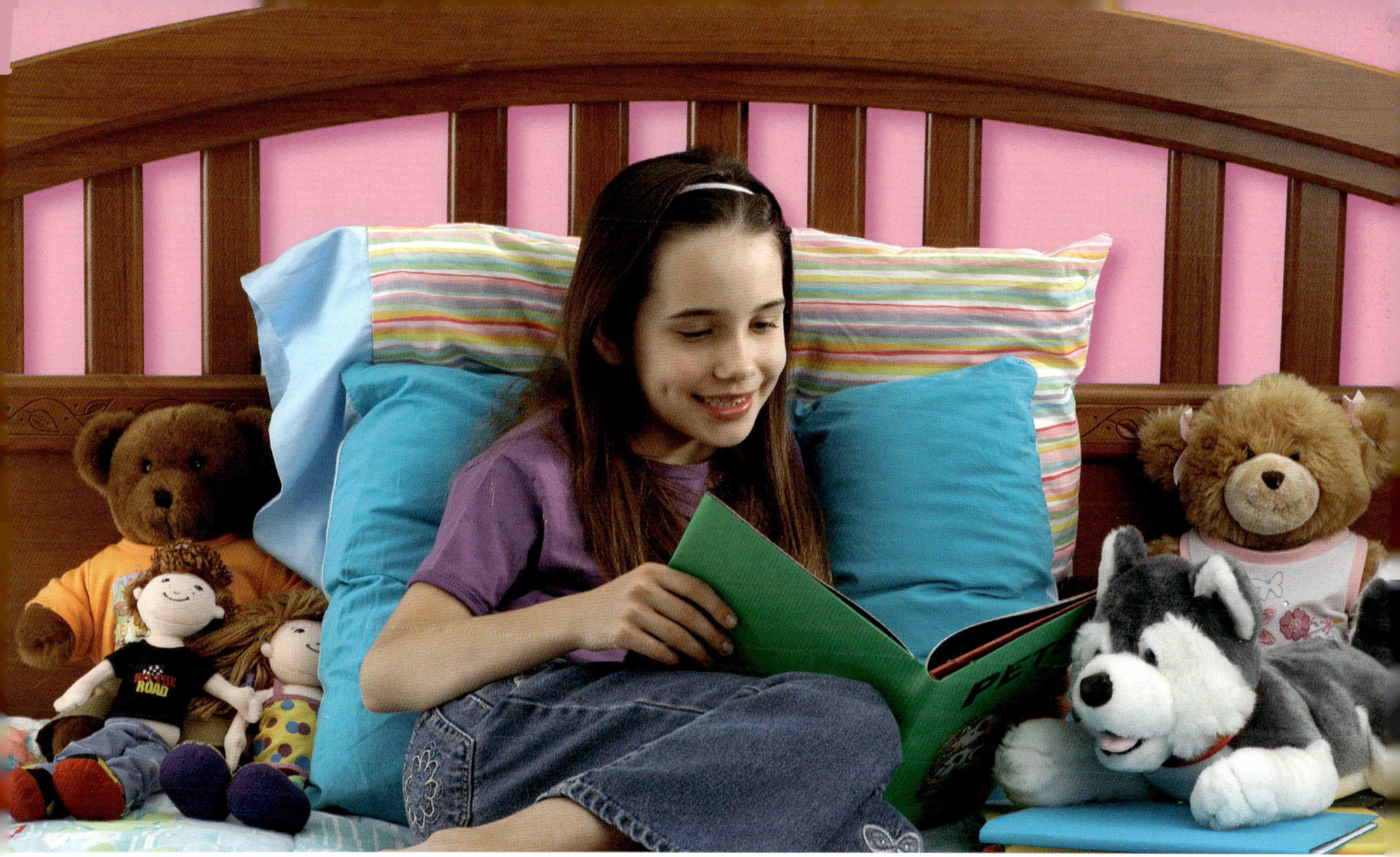

I love to read.

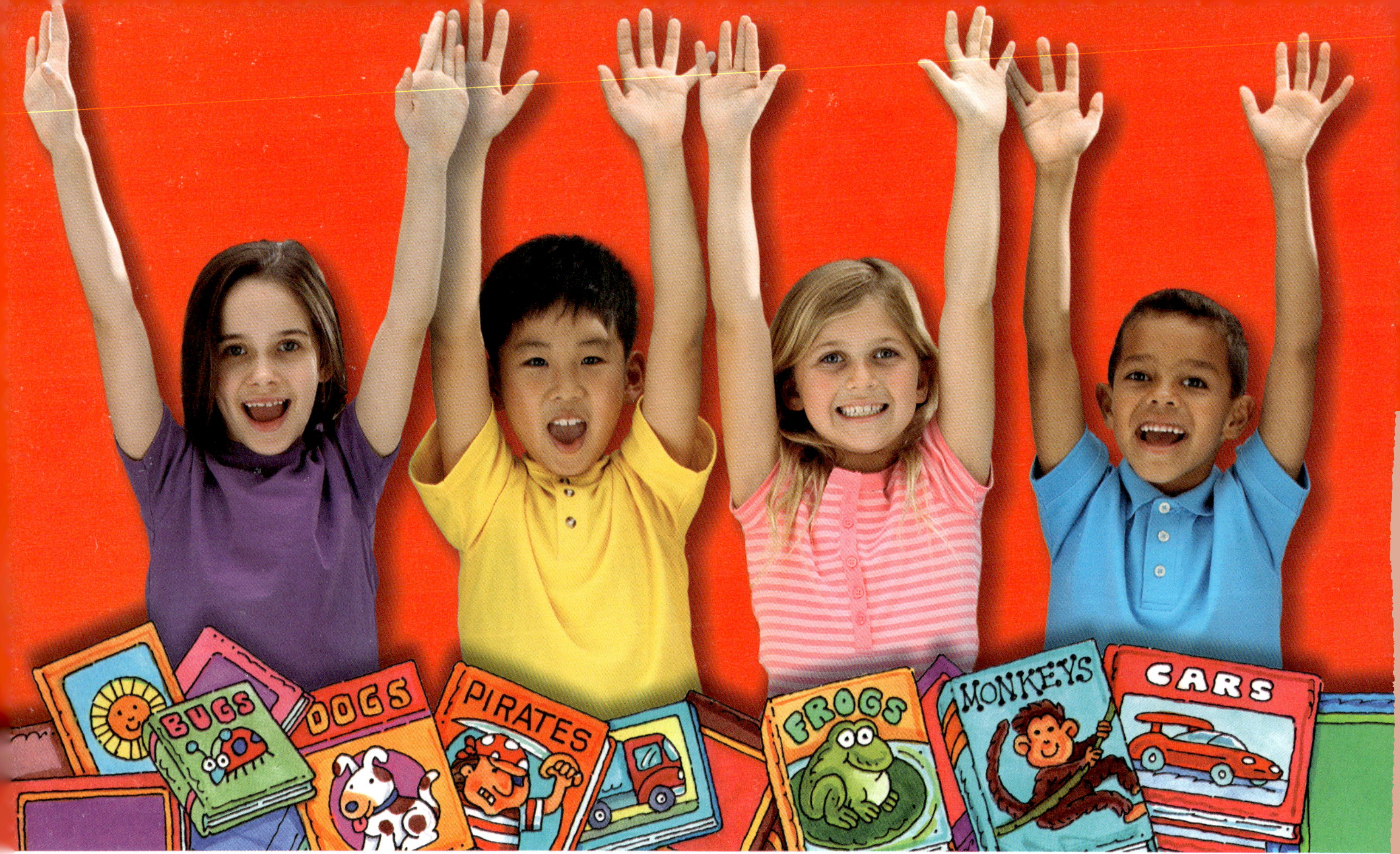

Reading is fun!